LIVING UPRIVER

LIVING UPRIVER

Artful Homes, Idyllic Lives

Text and photography by Barbara de Vries

Foreword by Emma Austen Tuccillo

RIZZOLI
NEW YORK

New York · Paris · London · Milan

Foreword

Emma Austen Tuccillo

I have always loved peering inside other people's homes. A ripple of excitement builds in my belly as I am welcomed through the front door and guided around sunny living rooms and warm kitchens with a kettle on or a meal cooking. I stare like a kid in a candy shop at art on the walls, a collection of magazines stacked in the corner, or patterned furniture that could be an heirloom. To me, homes are representations of personality, dreams, creativity—in a way that nothing else truly is. When it comes to setting up house in Upstate New York, I have found that the banks of the Delaware and Hudson Rivers and everywhere in between attract a certain kind of homesteader, a uniquely creative person who sees home as an act of individuality and a crucial starting point to building community.

That's what you will find in these pages. Homes that are vastly different yet wonderfully similar in their warmth, layering, and distinctness of character. They are microcosms, little worlds unto themselves, that reflect their owner's identities like mirrors. From a converted schoolhouse to a Greek Revival fixer-upper and an eighties ranch house with lots of potential, these homes inspire their owners to tap into their creativity, connect to nature, and build their dream life slowly and thoughtfully over time.

I have been lucky enough to visit some of the homes in this book through my company And North, a curated guide to Upstate New York. I have sat in the kitchen of Julie Hedrick and Peter Wetzler's converted church in Kingston and selected a teacup from a cupboard filled with hundreds, each uniquely patterned. I have lounged by the Scandinavian fireplace in Laura Chávez Silverman and George Billard's Eldred home while jam made from foraged berries bubbled on the stove. I have woken up in the guest room of Elizabeth Starks and Jake Sackett's Bovina home to the view of cows roaming on the snowy hillside in the distance, and I have scoured and sourced antiques in Ron Sharkey's barn, steps away from his columned home in Stone Ridge. From all these experiences, I can say that living Upstate is an opportunity—one to live a special kind of life that only you can dream up and a chance to host friends, find inspiration, and feel connected to your most creative and authentic self.

The homes you are about to explore have also led to incredible community building, forming invisible strings that connect the different towns and villages that dot the region. Without these Upstate homes, many businesses and connections would have never been forged, like Laura Chávez Silverman's Outside Institute, which connects people to the transformative powers of nature; Tom Roberts and Anna Aberg's Fly-Fishing Club and the home design studio that grew out of it, Homestedt; or Elizabeth Starks and Jake Sackett's supper series, which they host in the tavern below their home. For these individuals, home is a jumping-off point to new ideas and unknown places.

As you sit down to read this—ideally in a cozy, overstuffed chair by candlelight (if you're a romantic like me)—I hope it fills you with inspiration and invites you to see your own surroundings in a new way. Go inside these special homes with their front doors wide open, fire crackling in the next room, to explore not only someone's space but also their innermost self. Welcome. Stay awhile.

INTRODUCTION

Upriver

Living Upriver has roots in lockdown seclusion, when my husband, our three daughters, and I stayed home on our mountaintop in Milford, Pennsylvania. Like so many families, we came together after several years of going our own way. Our daughters Kiki and Leila were studying in the Netherlands and flew home when the pandemic suspended in-person classes. Iona, our eldest daughter, worked in film casting in New York City. I picked her up from her Brooklyn apartment a few days before the city shut down. To all of us, coming home meant being back in Milford. Reunited, we took turns cooking and baking, went on long nature walks in Delaware Water Gap National Park, celebrated holidays and birthdays with dance parties, adapted to remote working and studying, made art and books, shared stories at the end of each day, and appreciated the gift of being who we are together, as a family of adults.

When we eventually went down into the valley and fanned out across the Delaware River, we found a somewhat changed social landscape. The bond that my family and I had felt during lockdown stirred for others throughout the Pocono and Catskill Mountains, from the banks of the Delaware River to the shores of the Hudson River and everywhere in between and beyond. I had discerned this renewed sense of kinship on social media, and then I experienced it in person. People enjoyed simpler, cozier lives while sharing everything, which inspired new communities. A fresh web was being spun by those who'd already transitioned to country life—after 9/11, the 2009 stock market crash, Hurricane Sandy in 2012, or simply twenty-first-century city burnout—and also by those who'd escaped to their family's homes, weekenders, longtime locals, and first-time visitors. The lockdown emboldened them to find one another, online and on Zoom, and to exchange ideas about home making, cooking, gardening, parenting, home schooling, art, music, design, discoveries in nature, how to simplify, and staying true and sane—all with the urge to pioneer a larger utopian picture, and a new place called home. They made spare beds available to friends, luring them away from traumatized cities, promising nature, healthy living, wholesome food, and new connections. They created destinations that, once the pandemic subsided, would grow into new communities. And then, when the worst was over, they joined together for farm-to-table meals, nature walks, exhibitions, craft fairs, farmers markets, retreats, and more.

I call them the Sharing Generation. As toddlers at daycare, they learned to share their toys; as teenagers, they shared on social media; and, subsequently, the Sharing Generation has settled into a community-oriented way of life. Drawing from their own distinct talents, they embrace participation, trade resources, recycle possessions in circular economies, and establish new platforms for exchange. As you'll learn from the dynamic individuals featured in these pages, they also create inspired, welcoming spaces that express their personal styles. In addition to those in the book, countless people are a part of this vibrant and layered history.

After Hurricane Sandy left their New York City home condemned, Nhi Mundy and her husband, photographer Michael Mundy, moved to their weekend home in Sullivan County. They opened Bha and Me, a small chain of Vietnamese restaurants inspired by Nhi's grandmother's home cooking. They also created *Dveight*, a stylish newsprint magazine that unites the Upper Delaware region into a cohesive habitat of design-savvy pioneers. Kate Orne, a fashion photographer and curator with an impressive career in the city, moved upstate in 2009. Feeling a sense of isolation, she published *Upstate Diary*, a glossy biannual magazine that documents the homes, studios, and lives of artists, designers, and visionaries in the Hudson and Delaware River Valleys.

The Field + Supply makers market, where new settlers sell their home-crafted wares, started small in 2015, and now features two hundred vendors at its biannual event in Kingston. In 2022, Mexican artist Bosco Sodi and his wife, designer Lucia Corredor, who have a house in nearby Forestburgh, gutted an old Buick dealership in Monticello and created Assembly, a 23,000-square-foot museum. With no entry fee, it is an art resource in an otherwise underserved community.

Soul Fire Farm in Petersburg, New York, cofounded by environmental justice activist Leah Penniman, is an Afro-Indigenous community farm that produces and distributes fruit, vegetables, herbs, livestock, honey, and mushrooms to help end food apartheid. It also offers training programs for a new generation of farmers of color and shares stewardship of its land with the Stockbridge-Munsee Band of the Mohican Nation. The family-run Homestead School in Glen Spey, New York, has been at the center of the Upper Delaware community for over forty years, and its ideology—taking care of nature and one another—continues to embolden generations of alumni. Filmmaker Josh Fox and actor Mark Ruffalo introduced a movement against fracking to the Upper Delaware Valley community, which has since become a nexus for positive environmental change.

This legacy of environmental advocacy goes back as early as 1890, when the area attracted conservationist Gifford Pinchot, who's often called the Father of Forestry and became the twenty-eighth governor of Pennsylvania. Pinchot instigated the reforestation of the Upper Delaware and Hudson River regions after it had been decimated by logging industries in the nineteenth century. Grey Towers, his Milford home, a faux Normandy castle built in 1884, has since become the East Coast headquarters of the US Forest Service.

I bought my 1790 farmhouse in Milford in 1988. Initially, it was a weekend escape from my hectic life as a fashion designer on Seventh Avenue in Manhattan. I chose a place that, at the time, was unknown to the fashion crowd. I needed to be alone and at home in nature on weekends, wear overalls and rubber boots, and not care about how I looked. Over the past three decades, both Milford and I have changed. I married and had three daughters and, after 9/11, we moved to the farmhouse full-time. Our kids attended the Homestead School; we built an addition to the house; and we moved to Miami for the girls' high school years. My husband, Alastair, and I went back to Milford in July 2018, as the girls went to college. Milford's transition includes the addition of a great health food store and a farmers market, and the restoration of the legendary Hotel Fauchére, co-led by Sean Strub, our mayor, who continues to unite old and new ways of the town. There are annual film, music, and literary festivals and, during the pandemic, the adjacent Delaware Water Gap National Park attracted more nature lovers than ever before.

I am writing this on a cold day in February, watching the small silver waves of the Zaan River lapping below my window. I'm living about twenty miles upriver from Amsterdam, which is the last place I could have imagined when I started this book about artful homes and idyllic lifestyles upriver from New York City—originally called New Amsterdam. Last fall, just as I had finished photographing the final home in this book, my ninety-five-year-old mother fell sick, and I rushed to be with her in the Netherlands, the country of my birth. So now I live in two upriver homes: one urban, one country. I'm learning that nothing can be taken for granted. My family, my friends, and my idea of home. And as every day is unique, I learn from the rivers and try to go with the flow. I also take strength and inspiration from the people in this book, and the simple beauty they create—not only in their own lives but also in the lives of others. I hope you do too.

UPRIVER PIONEERS

Julie Hedrick and Peter Wetzler

Julie Hedrick, a Canadian-born painter, and Peter Wetzler, a musician and composer, discovered Kingston, New York, when they ran out of gas on their way back to the city, after taking Julie's paintings to a gallery in Toronto. "As we walked around the town, I could feel excitement building," Julie says. "The old buildings, the history, the Hudson River, and just this sense of enormous potential."

It was 1985. They were young artists living in a tiny East Village apartment and fantasizing about having lots of space to work, to stage concerts and exhibitions, and to create a community art center. When they stopped in Kingston, they called their only friend in the area, who happened to know of an enormous Baptist church, built in 1860, that had been for sale for a while. They saw it with a realtor that day; it felt like fate was guiding them. After some negotiations, Julie and Peter bought the church and its chapel, and moved in.

"We felt like pioneers," Julie says. "There were so many possibilities, but we had to start by honoring and restoring what was there." They saved the details around the chapel's windows and other architectural elements with historical materials; they restructured the courtyard by moving the original bluestone slabs and adding cobblestones; they treated the wood of the front door, staircase, and floors with Danish oil and painted some features white. "'Love it, honor it as it is, and play with it' was kind of our motto," Julie says.

Their vision for a creative community first materialized when, in 1987, Peter assembled the Repetos, an international music ensemble, to record albums and stage concerts at the church. For several weeks every year, the eight-member group and their families all lived at the church. "Many of them are from England, so that's how I got my collection of big teapots," Julie smiles.

Starting in 1989, Pauline Oliveros, a well-known American composer, used the church for a concert and, together with Peter, mentored and sponsored musicians from all over the world. Composer and sound artist Viv Corringham and others soon followed, establishing collaborations at the church and attracting more people to the area. "So many of our friends eventually bought homes here they called us the doulas of Kingston!" Julie says. In 2018, the City of Kingston presented Julie and Peter with a Distinguished Artists Award for their commitment to establishing a creative community.

In 2001, they separated the two properties and sold the church to friends who continue to run it as a studio, performance space, and art center. By 2010, the chapel had seven guest bedrooms and Peter, used to having people living with them, decided to add Airbnb to the house's operations—only he forgot to tell Julie. "One morning, he announced that our first Airbnb guests were arriving in the afternoon," Julie laughs. The *Church Des Artistes* B&B took off, and a steady flow of guests came and went until March 2020.

After one fastidious guest had departed, Julie decided to convert several closets into private bathrooms, one for each bedroom—seven in total. "I'm obsessed with clawfoot tubs," she says. "I found seven online, and Peter drove all over New England to pick them up. They just fit in his Prius."

During the pandemic, Julie and Peter mostly saw their children and a select "pod" of friends. They were content to use this more introverted time to focus on their work, but they were grateful when they could finally reemerge into their community and continue traditions like hosting a large Christmas dinner. "Maybe we won't have a hundred people this year, but we'll definitely get a good crowd," Julie says.

CHURCH
DES
ARTISTES
PLEASE RING
THE BELL

Julie and Peter's open front door is both beautiful and symbolic: over the years, they've welcomed friends who help with renovations and collaborate on creative projects, trading craft for community and friendship.

The couple sources seasonal vegetables, fruit, and poultry from farmers markets, a CSA and the Kingston YMCA Farm Project. They get bread from Jon's Bread, which grows its own rye and wheat and bakes in woodfired ovens.

Large communal meals do not have to be a cul nary challenge for the hosts. People love to brin food and be collaborators in the gathering c friends. Julie leaves it up to her guests to decid what dish to bring, rather than curating a potluc dinner.

Wild mushrooms do not need much cooking. Like most local fresh produce, they are full of flavor, and best when stir-fried in extra virgin olive oil, pepper, salt, a squeeze of lemon, and herbs from the garden.

Julie's table settings are an eclectic mix of dishes, crockery, and glasses collected over the years. The chairs are all different too—fitting for the guests, who are diverse, unique, and tell great stories.

Peter and Julie forage seasonal wild greens, lik nettles and mustard greens. Finely chopped mus tard greens are great in pesto; coarsely choppec they add flavor to frittatas.

Food and Friends

Sharing your home, Julie suggests, is the fastest way to make friends in a new place. "Coming together with food and music is how you create community," she says. "We are all really different, and what we have in common is a love of where we are."

Not long after they moved into the church, Peter went door to door and invited the entire neighborhood to join them for a Canadian Thanksgiving dinner, emulating Julie's family tradition. "It became the unofficial christening of the church," Peter says. Julie put all her art tables outside and soon they overflowed with food and drink that their guests brought: three turkeys, a baked ham, countless squashes, every kind of potato dish, salads, pastas, punch bowls, and at least a dozen pies. Neighbors met each other for the first time, and old stories of the town were shared. A sense of community was renewed, and the evening set the tone for how Julie and Peter's life in Kingston would unfold.

When they opened the B&B, breakfast became the focal point of their weekend cooking. "Our approach to everything, including food, is upsourcing—so the breakfast palate is determined by what's easily and locally available," Julie explains. In the early spring, they harvested wild knotweed and picked ramps, nettles, and wild mustard. For her famous B&B bread pudding, Julie included apples, pears, and peaches from the fruit trees in the courtyard.

Most years before the pandemic, they hosted a large community Christmas bash. Everyone sang around the piano, which they put in the middle of the great room. They moved the long harvest table into the courtyard, and Julie filled it with old cut-glass punch bowls. "You can buy those for nothing at Goodwill. I filled them with a strong hot punch of leftover fruit, alcohol, and juices," she says. "We also had fire pits with roaring fires. It was a magical inside-outside party."

HAND HEWN

Nadia Yaron and Doug Newton

Sculptor Nadia Yaron and fine metalworker Doug Newton knew by 2017 that they needed to escape Brooklyn. They'd outgrown their studios; their twins, Theo and Moon, were starting to walk; and they missed being in nature.

Doug, who grew up on thirty acres of forest in rural Ontario, is known for his custom bronze light fixtures, metal panels, and mirror frames, and counts Soho House and the Standard Hotel among his clients. Nadia was born in Brazil and moved to Long Island when she was six. In 2007, inspired by the combination of urban rawness and gentrification in Brooklyn—demolished interiors, scrapped furniture, and wooden waste—she crafted a collection of repurposed wooden furniture from found materials.

In 2014, continuing her quest for authenticity, Nadia collaborated with a textile group called Friends of Light, who develop their own natural yarns to spin and weave on traditional looms into no-waste couture jackets. "After the twins were born, I was still weaving all day," Nadia says, "but I just yearned to do something more physical." She took a class in woodcarving, but it proved restrictive. "I remember coming home and telling Doug that whatever I did, it had to be really big!" Nadia says, recalling her frustration. "I just told her that she needed to get a chainsaw and a large log," Doug laughs. When their neighbor took down a maple tree, Doug and Nadia collected logs that fit in their basement, and Nadia got to work with a battery-powered chainsaw. "While the girls were sleeping, I would bring down their baby monitor and start sawing," she says. "I was just chopping to discover possibilities."

In 2018, they heard about an affordable 160-year-old farmhouse that had come on the market not far from Hudson, New York. It was near good schools and a train station; it came with three barns: two for their studios and one for Nadia's parents. It had character and even a few acres of land.

When they finally moved in, in 2019, they realized it was also a fixer-upper. After a plumbing disaster, they took down a wall and accidently exposed a brick section with beautiful old wallpaper. "Downstairs felt like a maze. When Doug and I were in the kitchen, we had no idea where the girls were, so we took down more walls and removed doors. Now it flows together like one space," Nadia says. To brighten the rooms further, they stripped all the paint off the wooden moldings and treated the walls as if they were coated in nineteenth-century plaster. "I wanted to get the right texture, so I mixed one color in limewash and one color in fresco into this pale mineral green," Nadia says.

Nadia's parents converted one barn into an apartment and came to watch the girls while Nadia and Doug renovated the house and moved into their new studios. The pandemic made the family's introduction to country life a solitary experience and, when the twins started at a local Montessori school, they experienced a sense community for the first time. "Still, our days are pretty much the same, filled with kids and work, and there isn't time for much else," Nadia says, as she prepares for her first solo show at Francis Gallery, Los Angeles, in spring 2023. Doug supports her Herculean effort of creating large stone sculptures stacked with enormous pieces of wood by devising lifting and transportation systems.

Like hummingbirds, Theo and Moon flutter through the gardens, house, and studios, as if in constant search of exhilaration. They find it when a real hummingbird gets trapped in Nadia's barn, seeking an exit in the highest rafters. Doug, with endless patience, gently moves a long broom back and forth, inviting the hummingbird for a ride to freedom on its bristly surface. The girls peer up toward the beams and encourage it with pleas and squeals. Eventually, the hummingbird succumbs, takes a seat, and Doug gently coaxes it outside.

Ceramicist Paula Greif contacted Nadia for a collaboration using her porcelain and stoneware lamps and Nadia's hand-hewn sculpture. The two organic shapes make a handsome light fixture that gives off a soft suffused light.

Nadia and Doug whitewashed the interior walls of the studio over the original wood, creating different shades of wood. They left other panels, beams, and boards untreated. Paired with Nadia's sculptures, the effect is a patchwork of natural colors.

Nadia uses trees that have naturally fallen or wer struck by lightning, as well as found logs. She trie to grow back what she takes. Just this past year she planted 150 native hardwoods like maple, whit oak, black walnut, and cherry.

Kept on the entrance porch, Nadia's "chainsaw chair" is an early piece carved from one large log entirely by chainsaw, including the five "design" cuts in the back. She sanded the seat and legs to make them less prickly.

Sometimes Moon and Theo draw cloud shapes, then Nadia makes sculptures inspired by their drawings, and then the twins draw pictures of Nadia's cloud sculptures. They're perpetually inspired by one another.

Small sculptures made from wood and stone s on studio shelves. Nadia occasionally plays aroun with them, stacking them into new ideas, like a ta ble made of two rough-hewn arches and one long smooth piece.

Working with Wood

To transition from weaving textiles to working with wood, Nadia enlisted the help of a woodcarver, taking lessons focused on carefully whittling elaborate patterns in small pieces of wood. Nadia liked to carve but soon realized she was drawn to larger, organic gestures. When Doug suggested she try a chainsaw instead of a chisel, she embraced the idea. She started by creating wooden stools and tables from large logs. Because of her previous career in design, it felt natural to make utilitarian pieces, and she eventually made some of her own furniture after they moved into the farmhouse. Intuitively, she began by carving simple, almost primitive shapes and patterns, provoking a rawness that remains at the heart of her work.

Being back in nature inspires memories of her childhood in Brazil, lying under giant trees, playing with crystals, and holding handmade wooden objects. "My pieces were already sculptural, but being Upstate, I didn't want to think about function anymore. I wanted to explore shape and form," Nadia says of her transition to sculpture.

Her studio is bathed in southern light that streams in through a section of windows underneath the roofline, filling the space with soft diffused rays that not only bring out the various wood tones in the walls but hit the alabaster, quartz, and wooden sculptures from different angles, creating a play of glow, shadow, and texture. In winter, the studio has radiant heat; in the summer, Nadia works outside under a canvas shade sail. She works on several pieces at a time, making tall sculptures by stacking various elements, creating a dynamic effect between different colors and textures of wood on wood, stone on stone, or wood and stone. She often cuts directly into the wood or carves directly into the quartz, allowing the essence of the log or stone to guide its new form. Other times, she creates smaller sculptures as inspiration samples. "When I moved up here, everything got bigger, and it's still getting bigger," she says. "I want to go human size now."

FARM TO TABLE

Elizabeth Starks and Jake Sackett

Shortly after Elizabeth Starks and Jake Sackett met at Cornell University, they started picturing the life they would make together. Their dream came into focus when they traveled to Prague and fell in love with the countryside of the Czech Republic.

"We were hiking along a river and the trail led to a cluster of little homesteads where people welcomed us in to have a beer and a meal," Elizabeth says. "We stopped at one house that had this beautiful dining room and a husband and wife who cooked venison goulash and blueberry dumplings. It was one of those life-changing meals. We were like, 'How can we take this authenticity with us?'"

That romantic experience stayed with them, but replicating it at home took some time. After they graduated from Cornell, Jake went to law school and Elizabeth joined a start-up commercial brewery in Boston. "I learned how to brew and bottle beer," she says, "but working with people who were making their dream into reality was the most beneficial."

Not unlike their hikes in the Czech Republic, Elizabeth and Jake found inspiration during long walks in the woods around Concord, Massachusetts, a historic town with beautiful old homes. Every time they passed the Hartwell Tavern, built in 1733, they wondered if their future homestead could be based on its design. "I'm not kidding—we eventually returned with tape measures," Elizabeth admits.

The couple eventually sought land to build their version of a historic tavern and Czech home in Delaware County, New York, where Jake grew up and his forefathers farmed. "There were only two parcels on the market," Jake says. "One had no driveway, so we hiked up to the top pastures and saw the views down the valley, and kind of fell in love with it right there."

Following Elizabeth and Jake's direction, Elizabeth's father, a tech engineer and enthusiastic builder, helped create the blueprints for the house-tavern and barn-brewery. They broke ground in August 2019 and, two years later, the Bovina Fermentory hosted its first farm dinner. Eight years after their fateful trip to the Czech Republic, Elizabeth and Jake's dream came true: they were sharing farm-brewed beer, homecooked meals, and kindness with friends and neighbors.

To emulate the Hartwell Tavern, they used pine boards for the exterior of their home, staining them a deep brown color, and kept the interior design simple, with pale and neutral colors. They also used pine planks to cover the walls in the hallway, bathroom, dining hall, and shop, painting them in shades of white. "All the wood is from around here," Jake says. "It feels good to support a local mill, and they also make a beautiful product."

Together, Elizabeth and Jake built two big tables and the shelving units behind the bar, in the shop, and in the upstairs kitchen. Jake also crafted several window seats and benches that double as storage. "We followed Shaker-style design because it's simple, and the kind of woodwork Jake and I were able to tackle ourselves," Elizabeth says. The rest of their furniture was either thrifted or handed down by family and neighbors. "My grandpa kept all his milking stools, so we have many of those around," Jake says. "He also gave us the ceramic jugs from his dairy farm," Elizabeth adds. For a personal touch, Elizabeth designed a stencil and stamped a simple floral border on the wall of the guest bedroom, and added the same design to the downstairs utilitarian restaurant kitchen. "I would've gotten carried away, but Jake stopped me from stamping the whole thing," she says, "but for our future house I can see myself doing a wallpaper."

The entire tavern building will eventually become an inn with guest bedrooms in the upstairs space that Elizabeth and Jake now occupy. They're already planning a new home for themselves, in the back of the property, where they'll continue to dream and plan their future.

Hotpoint

BOVINA
FARM AND FERMENTORY
LOUISE
TABLE BEER
WITH LEMON
3.4 %
ALC / VOL

Elizabeth and Jake found the wood-paneled bar on Craigslist; it used to be a general store counter in Maine. It took a U-haul and a daytrip to collect and was raised several inches for its new life as the tap bar in the dining hall.

For Valentine's Day dinner, dessert was an apple strudel made with local apples, hazelnuts, cranberries, cardamom, and cinnamon, served with whipped crème fraîche from local dairy cream and maple syrup.

Bouquets are made from wild apple blossom bluebells, and daffodils in the spring; daisies, fern and daylilies in the summer; sunflowers, chrysar themums, and dahlias in the fall; and grasses, drie milkweed, and thistles in the winter.

A sweet potato and local goat cheese dish from a four-course menu. The sweet potatoes were roasted in house beer and sprinkled with sea salt, pepper, chopped chives, and basil, and served with Louise, a light table beer with lemon.

Bovina Fermentory focuses on two categories of beers: light, easy-drinking lagers and mixed fermentation beers made with unique yeasts and bacteria that create a more complex flavor. The beers are fermented and aged in wine barrels.

Jake and Elizabeth built the large tables along th side of the dining hall; Elizabeth's father built th window seats. The farm tables came from Jake relatives, and the folding chairs came from loc thrift stores and are kept on pegs on the wall.

Creating Community

The Bovina Farm and Fermentory is Elizabeth and Jake's "shared home." On most Saturdays, the first-floor dining room opens to thirty-four guests for a communal dinner that Elizabeth and Jake prepare and serve themselves. "People arrive at six thirty and we spend the evening together over four courses that are paired with our home-brewed beer," Elizabeth says. The dinners are tailored to the season. In summer, the tap room and lawn are open Friday through Sunday, and two special feasts with a fire pit and grilled meat, in June and September, take place at long tables under the stars. In winter, the dining room is candlelit, intimate, and often surrounded by snow. In summer and fall, they serve produce from their own gardens and from local farms, which also supply them with meat, poultry, and dairy. In winter and spring, they source locally as available and keep supplies in a cold storage cellar built in the hillside below the house. They've been expanding their livestock by adding dairy sheep and two donkeys to their flocks of ducks, geese, and chickens, and are planning bigger vegetable plots to grow more of their own produce for the coming summer season.

Jake does most of the cooking, often inspired by old family recipes, while Elizabeth focuses on accoutrements. Jake is also the brewer, and Elizabeth is an accredited cicerone. Together, they collaborate on the flavors and recipes of the beers that are paired with the different courses. "Some people say that they're not beer drinkers, but often, by the end of the evening, they tell us how much they enjoyed all four of our brews," Jake says.

They don't advertise and instead rely on word of mouth and shared Instagram posts to attract guests who understand and enjoy the concept of a dinner party experience in an intimate home setting. In their own way, Elizabeth and Jake are creating a community of like-minded people. Guests keep returning, often introducing new friends. "It's not commercialized, but we're always fully booked," Elizabeth says. "They're coming to our house, and it's just the two of us—maybe it's not for everybody, but enough people seem to enjoy what we do."

RESTORED REVIVAL

Ron Sharkey

"I was looking for farmhouse modern, but got Greek Revival," says Ron Sharkey. After living in a small, secluded cottage in Accord, New York, for almost two decades, Ron started looking for a home near Rhinebeck or Kingston. He found one in Stone Ridge, one of his favorite towns. He also got more than he bargained for.

"When I bought it, I thought it was a kind of cupcakey little folly," he says. "Now it's almost four thousand square feet. I should have measured it." But the house ticked a lot of Ron's boxes. In addition to its location, it had two barns that were small enough to manage his antiques business by himself, and it had enough potential to unleash his passion for creating beautiful spaces.

The lower level of the ramshackle Greek Revival originally had a huge brick fireplace and a small kitchen, and the rest had been left as an unfinished basement. Upstairs, everything was painted peach. A fan of period English interiors, Ron liked the idea of creating an upstairs-downstairs feeling, with a utilitarian lower level and more formal floors above, like a traditional country manor house. "I call the small downstairs bedroom the 'cook's room,' but of course, I have never had a cook," he laughs. "Then it became the bedroom where I sleep most of the time." He used the bluestone slab from a walkway to the street to create the floor in the fireplace room. He raised the floor of what became the dining room, using leftover boards that he found in the porch attic. And he created a black-and-white "Vermeer floor" in the kitchen, using closeout tiles.

Ron's transition to living in the countryside was gradual. In the mid-eighties, he worked at an alternative high school in New York City as an art and English as a Second Language (ESL) teacher. "It was a great program for immigrant kids who didn't speak English yet," he says. Around the same time, he started spending vacations with friends in Cape Cod. "During the time that AIDS was claiming a lot of lives, Provincetown became a very supportive community," Ron says. He considered buying a home near Provincetown when another friend invited him to spend the weekends at his restored farm in Upstate New York. Initially, Ron was relieved to get back to the city on Sunday evenings but, eventually, he began looking for a place of his own. "It made more sense to buy Upstate, two hours outside New York City, than on the Cape," he says.

Ron found the cottage in Accord in 1995 and, in 2005, he opened his first antique store. As the business became sustainable, he bought an old barn in the center of nearby High Falls, painted it black, and named it the Black Barn. It became a popular destination for a new generation of weekenders and full-time residents, not least because of recurring Field and Barn fairs he held on the front lawn. Ron's collaboration with interior designer Brad Ford has evolved into the now widely successful biannual Field + Supply Makers Market in Kingston, New York.

The Stone Ridge house is a testament to Ron's evolution in design, like an expression of something he's been dreaming about for a long time. Each space has its own identity, yet it feels like the same family has roamed the house for a century. When I ask Ron about his enormous collection of *World of Interiors* magazine, he tells me he first subscribed when he got the Accord cottage. "Sometimes I couldn't even open them. They were just so beautiful!" he says. He kept them all when he moved, bundled them up by year, and left them in the hallway waiting for built-in bookshelves or even their own library. Instead, the temporary stacks have become more like an art installation—an homage to inspiration. When Ron's Accord cottage was featured in *World of Interiors* in 2014, Ron was both stunned and thrilled. "I am eternally grateful to photographer Don Freeman for making that dream come true," he says.

SCANDINAVIAN DESIGN
THE ENCYCLOPEDIA OF FURNITURE
A HOME OF YOUR OWN
Shades of COUNTRY
Country Wisdom • David Larkin
The Shopkeeper's Home Caroline Roseland
HOUSES of GREENWICH VILLAGE

INTERIORS
INTERIORS

ICE WATER

Some pieces need a little TLC. Ron cleans, polishes, and makes small repairs. A local carpenter assists him with more complicated restorations and, occasionally, they reassemble damaged pieces and use parts from one piece to restore another.

The White Barn and the Garden Shed are open on weekends throughout spring, summer, fall, and winter until the Christmas holidays. During the week, Ron opens it by appointment or if he happens to be around.

Rather than using Airbnb to generate income from the spare rooms on the third floor, Ron lists his property with a location agency for photo and film shoots.

Seasonal flowers and plants are part of the white barn's and garden shed's decor. Sometimes, Ron sells fresh and dried flowers, sprigs, twigs, plants, and arrangements he's created from the garden.

A painting can set the mood of a room. Ron applies this not only throughout his own home but also to the paintings he sells in the store, keeping the design of a parlor, bedroom, or kitchen in mind.

Ron uses instinct when buying antique and vintage pieces. When he creates an interior, he draws on his experience in composition and form, and lets the house, or its rooms, dictate what is needed.

Repair and Upcycle

From an early age, Ron collected paraphernalia from thrift stores. Following visits to Provincetown, he'd store his finds in his small apartment on Sixteenth Street in Manhattan. "I'd keep it in my closets and under my bed, hoping that one day I could flip it." The time came when, in the mid-eighties, he took a stall at the famous Chelsea Flea market in Manhattan.

Today, as a collector and reseller, Ron sees possibility in damaged vintage furniture if it has a workable resale value once it's been restored. He knows a piece's value from decades of experience, but still looks for markings that indicate its origins. Telltale signs are often in the condition of the wood underneath or inside, the quality and age of the nails and screws, and the presence of dovetail joints. Then he decides whether the damaged piece is worth the effort and cost to restore it into an attractive sellable piece.

Ron suggests following your instinct when buying vintage pieces and keeping the space you're furnishing in mind. If you're thinking of restoring to retail, start small by finding things at thrift stores, yard sales, and auctions, and selling them to friends, online, or at markets.

Ron opened his first store in 2005 and has continued to grow his business ever since. To keep his inventory exciting and relatively affordable—even at a time when colleagues say the good stuff is disappearing—Ron relies on various sources, including friends and individuals who go to him first. "I also scour estate sales, auctions, barn sales and yard sales, other antique shops and cooperatives, small and large flea markets, and even Facebook Marketplace," he says.

As many new, creative young people move to the area full-time his customer base has changed to include hotels like Audrey's Farmhouse, in Wallkill; Inness, in nearby Accord; and Hasbrouck House, on Stone Ridge's Main Street. And decorators and other talented individuals rely on Ron's curated inventory to help furnish their rooms. "They're all very lovely and have great taste, which keeps me on my toes," he says.

UPSTATE SWEDISH

Anna Aberg and Tom Roberts

Anna Aberg spent much of her childhood in the countryside near Gothenburg, Sweden, and Tom Roberts grew up in northern England and Scotland, and so it isn't surprising that they felt at home in the foothills of the Catskills, with its rugged farmland and endless forests, waterfalls, and streams.

While still working nine-to-five jobs in New York City, Anna and Tom went Upstate whenever they could, renting various cabins, farmhouses, and converted barns. "We would be sitting around the fire, dreaming up plans and looking at real estate online," Tom says. "Eventually, we found these two very dilapidated, almost terrifying looking buildings on the edge of Livingston Manor." The property contained six hundred feet of New York's Willowemoc Creek, the famous fly-fishing river that connects Livingstone Manor and Roscoe.

"Over the first six months, a gaggle of friends who were excited at trading a keyboard for a sledgehammer, shovel, or paintbrush helped us out," Tom says. In addition to restoring the house, Anna and Tom were also constructing dining tables, tents, and a sauna on the river. When they completed the work, they invited their helpers to enjoy the fruits of their labor. At the celebration, everyone realized that other friends would also love a Livingstone Manor fly-fishing experience.

"It was always meant as a house for ourselves with a view to creating a space to share with friends," Anna says. The success of the "Fly-Fishing Club" came as a bit of a surprise and forced them to rethink their lives in the city. They were creating a year-round destination, a bed-and-breakfast nature retreat of sorts, with not only fly-fishing but hiking trails, saunas, outdoor cooking, and cozy indoor living spaces.

Once they'd committed to the country full-time, Anna and Tom needed more space for themselves and bought a small Victorian house nearby, which they named the Lady Pomona. In no time, it became a bed-and-breakfast too, and they were on the lookout again. "We realized that we needed to create a more sustainable life for ourselves, a home of our own, and not something we capitalized," Anna says. Meanwhile, many regular guests bought their own properties and came to Anna and Tom for help with the renovation, design, and decorating of their new homes. This led to Homestedt, Anna and Tom's studio for their budding interior design business and a store for their favorite home goods.

Driving home one day, only minutes away from Lady Pomona, Tom spotted a new "For Sale by Owner" sign. "I knew Anna was walking our dog, Biscuit, on the trail behind the property, so I called her and was like, 'Get in the car. I found our next home,'" he says. A few minutes later, they pulled up to an old ranch house with vinyl siding. "It was ugly and suffocated by trees, but it had this beautiful stream running by it," Anna says. They ultimately gutted the ranch house up to the roof and down to the foundation, changing its identity entirely.

Whereas their first two historic properties were inspired by the British country homes of Tom's youth—old beams, wallpaper, antiques, traditional paintings, leather couches, and dark wooden floors—the new house was inspired by Anna's roots. "Tom always liked the Scandinavian aesthetic, and I really wanted pale wood on the walls," Anna says. After some searching, they found a local lumberyard that would mill their planks to size using affordable basswood. "We've somehow managed to create a Scandinavian-Japanese minimalist space inside a North American ranch house," Tom laughs.

The walls of paneled windows, open spaces, and neutral furniture emphasize the seasons as they evolve around the house—from the cool brightness of spring to the deep green of summer, the rich foliage of fall, and the whiteness of winter.

"I no longer have the urge to leave in the morning," Anna says, "It feels like I'm already outside."

SORRY –
TEMPORARILY
OUT OF SERVICE

An old pantry cupboard was repurposed as a linen cabinet for the Boarding House at Seminary Hill. Selecting antique or vintage furniture to create a lived-in, homey feeling is part of Anna and Tom's design process.

Each unit at the Boarding House has a kitchenette with painted wooden shelves, wainscoting, and pegs. The countertops are made from reclaimed wooden slabs, and rustic linen curtains hide the pots and pans below.

Adding a bathtub to a bedroom creates a fee ing of intimacy. The alcove in this bedroom at th Boarding House was a perfect fit for a salvage claw-foot tub. Keeping the faded paint on a vintag tub gives a historic patina to a renovated room.

For the natural wood-paneled walls in their home, Anna and Tom chose locally milled basswood, a light, soft wood, rather than white oak, a more expensive hardwood. They added accents like found antlers, unique light fixtures, and ceramics.

For some of the woodwork and the furniture at the Boarding House, Anna and Tom used different shades of greenish-blue Farrow and Ball paints to create a harmonious, vintage color palette throughout the two buildings.

For his tiny home office, Tom used maps of Nort America as wallpaper and decorated it with Catskill Mountains flag, a Mountie hat, and an em broidery sampler that reads: "the ornaments of house are the friends who frequent it."

Making House

As a result of their seemingly boundless creative energy, Anna and Tom's business evolved from Airbnb hospitality to a significant design studio that restores and builds homes. Homestedt's first big design project was the Boarding House at Seminary Hill, a boutique hotel in the former Callicoon General Hospital, which had been derelict for some time. They gutted both buildings, reimagined the rooms with private bathrooms and kitchenettes, and created interiors that feel authentic and homey.

In an ongoing quest to create the perfect place, using the experience of restoring a dozen local homes, Anna and Tom designed the Homestedt House, a partially modular structure that comes in several sizes and layouts and can be built within six months. "We're building the first one on a mountain, with really great views and access to a lake," Tom says.

The two-bedroom house is about 1,600 square feet and has a vaulted open plan living room. Unlike the traditional design of Seminary Hill, the house is a mix of Japanese and Scandinavian minimalism. In contrast to the pale wood of their own house, they used black *shou sugi ban* burnt wood for the siding. And they added the warm and distinctive interior design touches for which they're known.

They credit their success not least to their full-time crew. "To get the right quality is often a question of precision and patience," Anna says, "and we've learned a lot from each other."

In a search for a space large enough to consolidate their growing business under one roof, Anna and Tom came across the dormant North Branch Cider Mill, one of the oldest cider mills in the area. After several months of negotiations, they bought the compound. "We plan to fire up the old cider-making equipment and have an American-English-Swedish-style café in the mill," Anna says.

They also plan to create an expanded retail space for the Homestedt collection of homeware, and furniture. Their design studio will go into the three-story barn, and they'll use a full carpentry-making space to build custom furniture for the store and design projects. "There might be a couple goats and other livestock—and possibly some saunas and a bath house on the river," says Tom.

GRAPHIC FARMSTEAD

Carin Goldberg and James Biber

Carin Goldberg, a graphic designer, and James Biber, an architect, have moved back and forth between New York City and Stanfordville, New York, since the mid-eighties. Among the benefits of having a home Upstate, James explains, is that "in the city, no matter where I started on a Saturday or Sunday, I always found myself back at the office, working, and that was irritating for both Carin and me. At our place Upstate, I was at least working on my own house instead of other people's homes."

They found the house when they walked into a realtor's office on a whim, after visiting a friend in Millbrook. They gave the agent a vague description of the kind of fixer-upper they had in mind and fell in love with the first place they saw: an 1820 farmhouse on a knoll overlooking two ponds, surrounded by twenty acres of sweeping fields and forest.

"The house was tiny, and we never figured out how a family with five kids had lived there before us," James says. They added a porch facing the pond and updated the kitchen and bathroom. After a giant water snake crossed Carin's path while she was swimming in the pond, they built a swimming pool.

In the nineties, when their son, Julian, was little, they moved to the farmstead full-time, where he attended a local Montessori school. When it was time for Julian to attend high school, the city became appealing once more, and they moved to Brooklyn. "We kept the house Upstate, but as Julian had things like soccer practice, we didn't go up anymore," James says. They considered selling the house, but things shifted in 2014, when Carin was awarded the Rome Prize for design and spent six months as a fellow at the American Academy in Rome. "That year changed the way I thought about what I wanted to do with my life," she says. "And when I came back, I went from doing commercial graphic design to making art." Instead of selling the farmhouse, they made it their full-time home once again, expanding the house by adding a studio for each of them, a large bedroom suite, and a comfortable guest room. "I told James I didn't want that thing architects do, where there's this old house and then there's this startling new building next to it," Carin says. The original structure had been an 1800s schoolhouse that was moved to the current site to function as a small farmstead.

James had considered a modern approach to the expansion but, after Carin's input, he figured it would be more interesting to design a three-part composition of the old house: one slightly more modern and then another even more modern, creating three linked pavilions with equal roof lines. "I got around the old-new architect trope by giving each a slightly different character," James says. The old house with the porch sits at the front, with the living room and original fireplace on the ground floor. The staircase leads to the former second floor, which now has a large guest room and some closet space. The middle part of the addition has a large kitchen and a new entry with a mudroom on one side and a sunroom on the other. The third structure has a studio-library on the ground floor. The new second floor has a studio-office, large bedroom suite with a dressing room, and connecting bathroom.

James has an aversion to drywall because it's overused for its efficiency. "It just turns everything into the same kind of house," he says, "so upstairs we used painted wood paneling. It feels more natural, and the gaps between the planks are always a little different, as they shrink at different rates."

By keeping the proportions similar throughout the house, James ensured that the flow of new and old feels organic and respectful of the home's history. He did, however, give a nod and a wink to Carin's and his modern, graphic aesthetic by exposing the steel beam of the third structure and painting it bright red.

RICARD
BERGER
PASTIS
51
TUNA FISH &

AM
YPE

Do it
LE CORBUSIER LE GRAND
LE CORBUSIER LE GRAND
MONUMENTALE
BAUHAUS
SAT-MON-TUE

SIBLEY BIRDS

TO
PAINT
SIGNS
New Japanese Archi
FOOD RU
LADIE

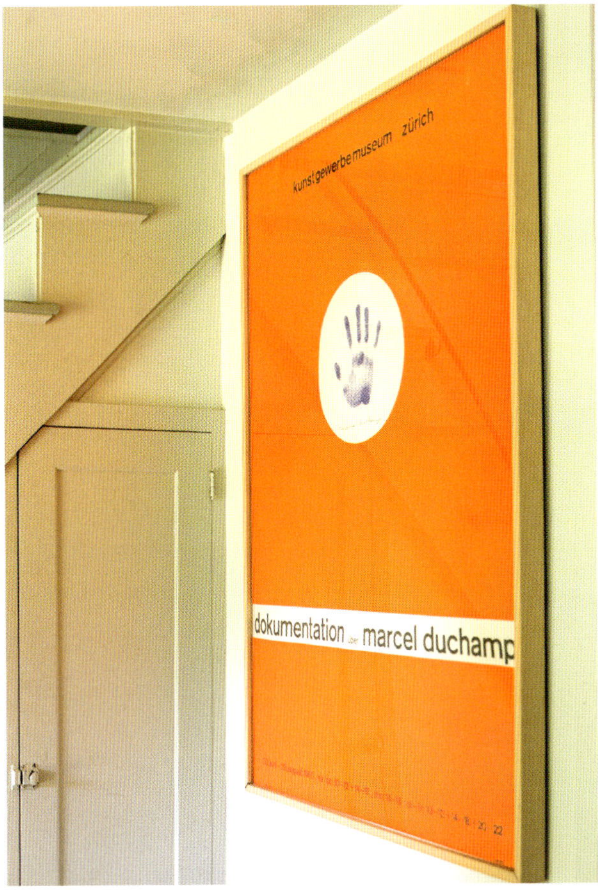
kunstgewerbemuseum zürich
dokumentation
marcel duchamp

kitchen

The coat rack in the glass mudroom is a graphic design expression right at the entry to the home with coats, hats, boots, and bags in bold colors and patterns that are visible from outside the house.

The steel beam that supports the cantilevered second floor is a modern exclamation point, a visual surprise, in contrast to the otherwise subtle design of the new addition.

Colorful accents throughout the house are ofte combined with Carin's work, or with art created b friends and colleagues. These casual design ges tures add a feeling of creative spontaneity.

The flowers in the garden are minimal and chosen for the strong effect of their color and structure. A perfect configuration of giant purple allium at the bottom of stone steps appear to point the way to the entrance of the house.

The ground-floor studio contains James and Carin's library of design, art, and architecture books, which they've collected over several decades. The shelves are also dotted with clever tableaux that combine graphic design with witty knickknacks.

The bathroom consists of two separate space that connect two bedrooms by three bright pock et doors. The pink, green, and blue panels create unique appearance and are rarely left in the sam configuration.

Mixing His and Hers

Carin, a well-known graphic designer who started her career designing album covers for CBS Records, is decidedly two dimensional. James, an architect who has worked with design firms like Pentagram, works in three dimensions.

The graphic quality of the farmstead interior isn't from only the posters and their taste in art but also from the colored square tiles covering the kitchen floor, the use of patterned fabric, and the use of color. Before the renovation, Carin and James filled the house with whatever style they were into at any given time. "Over thirty-odd years, you can imagine how many personal fads we've gone through," James says. They used to cover every single surface with art but, after the renovation, they left more negative space. They also curated their collection of furniture by choosing only the best of everything they loved—from early American and Shaker to mission and mid-century. The resulting interior is a perfect combination, as a result of their impeccable taste and mutual attraction to bold and graphic statements.

Carin and James also use their distinct talents to contribute to community and family. During the 2016 elections, they found the local Democratic Party's yard signs to be particularly jarring—so, Carin, who designed Madonna's debut album cover, offered to design the campaign for the local party chapter.

When Carin was finishing her fellowship in Rome, James was working on adding a black wall to the bedroom closet. "She'd been making white pastel drawings on black paper, and I hoped that, eventually, she'd draw on it," James says. "So, originally, the wall was like a blank canvas." But when James built the bookshelves in the library-studio, they needed a place to put Carin's art that had been on the walls. "It would have been just crazy to take her drawings to the basement and never look at them again," he remembers. So, while she was out, James took a hammer and nails and covered the black wall with thirty-six of Carin's drawings. "When she saw it, she was overwhelmed," he says. "Her work is beautiful, and I'm happy it's there. And so is she."

LIVING GREEN

Todd Carr and Carter Harrington

Todd Carr and Carter Harrington jumped into living Upstate with all four feet—and almost leaped right out when winter came, overwhelmed by subzero temperatures, blizzards, and isolation.

Soon after they met, in 2015, they rented a summer cottage in Oak Hill, New York, about thirty minutes northwest of Hudson. "We made some friends and, when August came, we didn't want to go back to the city," Carter says. "Then September came, and our friend Lucinda Mellen told us about a little 1850 farmhouse that was for sale down the road." When they realized the purchase price was close to their annual rent in the city, they threw caution to the wind, bought the house, drove back to the city, piled what they could into their car, and moved Upstate. "By November, the dreamy phase of, 'Oh my God, we own a house!' quickly dissolved into, 'Okay we need to face reality and pull it together because winter is coming.' We were like, 'Oh my gosh, what have we done?'" Carter says.

Carter has a background in interior design and fabrication, and Todd is a master gardener, stylist, and ceramicist. In their early days Upstate, without a plan, they initially lived on savings, then Todd did some work for a local artist. Together, they worked briefly as "lifties" at the local ski mountain. In spring, they decided to get serious about renovating the old farmhouse and try something new by combining their talents to create a mixed retail and art space. Again, they told Lucinda about their plan, and she showed them an empty 1869 carriage barn on her property. "It was a powerful space," Carter says. "The raw wood of the floors and walls even felt a little Japanese."

Todd had owned an antique store in Maine, still had vintage furniture in storage, and imagined a mix of botany, antiques, and horticulture-inspired pottery. They named the space Hort and Pott and, by the summer, they'd transformed the old carriage house into a popular retail destination. "The following December, Todd made a beautiful wreath and posted it on social media, and the response was huge," Carter says. "This focused us, and we replaced most of the antiques with botanicals."

Back at the farmhouse, Todd planted an extensive garden, which became another source of inspiration for the carriage house. The subsequent visual storytelling of their social media posts evoked an idyllic life—from farmhouse to garden to studio to home—that people wanted to see, touch, and experience. "I love it when people pick up on something," Todd says about the botanical environments they craft. "It definitely brings out emotions in people," Carter adds.

As they outgrew the carriage house, Carter and Todd started looking for a place where home, studio, gardens, and gallery would integrate organically. They found the perfect property in Freehold, just fifteen minutes from the carriage house. It included a Victorian house with twelve rooms, a former boarding house, two outbuildings, and a stream, all on twenty acres of land. "The property had been through many incarnations, and the buildings were in different stages of neglect," Carter says. "So when things slowed down in 2020, we started by renovating the boarding house, and reopened in the summer."

The big house was a complete gut job. "The potential is enormous, but we're restoring it in a very Hort and Pott way, sourcing vintage pieces, staying authentic, and layering elements that normally take years to evolve," Carter says.

With Todd as the artist in his studio and Carter the maker in his workshop, they've created more than a nursery, flower shop, or gallery. To them, horticulture is an essential part of life, presented in a dense green environment that helps people reimagine the way they live inside versus outside. "It's all about understanding how to bring nature inside any time of year," Carter says.

OFFICE OF...
TOWN CLERK & TREASURER
BRADLEY, MAINE

Objects new and old, made on-site, found, or thrifted dot the yard and gardens. They serve as inspiration or as props for creating compelling imagery in Hort and Pott's storytelling.

Materials for landscaping and cultivating the gardens fill the work shed, from bags of soil, manure, and peatmoss, to shovels, pots, and heavy machinery like a concrete mixer and a new utility vehicle.

Todd leaves sculptural concrete castings from tree trunks and large exotic leaves outside the casting studio to dry. Unique hand castings are an iconic part of Hort and Pott's collection.

Remnants of Victorian wallpaper cover much of the old boarding house. Todd and Carter kept the original wallcovering and embellished it with a wreath stamp and lath from demolished walls at the Little Red Farmhouse.

Hort and Pott is a gallery, laboratory, studio, greenhouse, and home all at once. The space incorporates nature in both craft and space and inspires visitors to take a similar sensibility home, and to be creative outdoors.

Todd grows or forages most of his botanical materials on the property. Using flowers, grasses branches, seedpods, acorns, thistles, and winterberry throughout the year, he defies tradition by artfully combining fresh and dried plant matter.

Bringing Nature Indoors

When gathering vegetation in the wild for homemade bouquets, wreaths, or other arrangements, it's important to cut modestly, allow room for regrowth, and leave no trace.

Before Carter and Todd had their own twenty acres, they would explore on old dirt roads and forage botanicals from roadside abundance. Now they go out in their utility vehicle and cultivate their own land. "We're lucky that our land has a diverse ecosystem, with a pond and wetlands, meadows, and a pine forest. We have access to lots of different materials," says Todd. For his holiday wreaths, he visits his parents' farm in Pennsylvania to gather spruce, winterberry, and willow. He listens to the seasons and the weather to scale what and when he cuts. "Todd has taught me how gardeners are engaged in a constant conversation with their surroundings and take notice of nature's fluctuations," Carter says.

Heading into fall, they cut and prepare large batches of dried flowers like hydrangeas, leaving long stems and removing the leaves, which they compost. Next, they bundle them in differing lengths, wrap a rubber band around the base, and hang the batches upside down from the rafters in Todd's studio, where they dry for several weeks. Milkweed pods, one of their favorites, are structural and make great containers for Todd's vignettes. "Before we pick the pods, we let the milkweed run its course. We spread the seeds where they grow, to ensure abundance next year," Todd explains.

Todd takes a length of forest grapevine as the base for his wreaths and twists it into a circle until he is happy with its shape and volume. Next, he adds dried material like spruce, dried grass, and winterberry. The natural shape of these wild elements inspires the design direction of the wreath. Then he layers in other elements like pine cones, acorns, dried flowers, and berries—and even feathers, dried citrus, ribbon, and small vintage ornaments.

"Creating vignettes and incorporating live plant material with dried elements, other fibers, or Carter's concrete vessels, and then weaving it all together, brings me ultimate joy," Todd says.

AUDREY'S FARMHOUSE

Sally Watkinson and Doug Posey

When Sally Watkinson met Doug Posey, they were living in the same building in Portland, Oregon. Not long after they began dating, Sally became director of visual merchandising for a fashion retailer in New York City. Rather than settle for a long-distance relationship, Doug, a finance lawyer, also took a job in New York and went with Sally across the country.

From their small Brooklyn apartment, they fantasized about an idyllic, self-sufficient life outside the city. Scanning real estate ads, Doug came across Audrey's Farmhouse—a turnkey bed-and-breakfast near New Paltz in a 1740s farmhouse with five bedrooms, an owner's cottage, and an impressive rental calendar. "I wasn't sure about it," Sally says, "but Doug has this big entrepreneurial spirit and isn't afraid of failing."

The first six months weren't easy. Sally still worked in the city four days a week while Doug lived in the owner's cottage Upstate. On weekends, they hosted and cooked elaborate breakfasts for guests: bicycling enthusiasts, dog owners, and others who'd been coming to Audrey's for years. Back in Brooklyn, Sally conceptualized the new look of the farmhouse by creating Pinterest boards and sharing them with Doug. She'd spent many childhood summers at her aunt's old stone home in the English countryside and wanted to evoke the feeling of her family's heritage—antique heirlooms, Persian rugs, fireplaces, big breakfasts in cozy kitchens, muddy boots, wet dogs, and people coming and going. "After buying the farmhouse, we didn't have much money left," Sally says, "so it was all about restoring old things back to life and being creative with our budget."

It wasn't long before they started contemplating the vacant commercial nursery across the street from the farmhouse: its vast glass greenhouse would make a fabulous event space, the sheds could become guest rooms, there was space for parking, and the views of Shawangunk Ridge were incredible. So they decided to expand. "The whole point was to continue what we loved doing, but on a viable scale," Doug says. Sally quit her job, their first child was born, and they started the new project by replacing the old greenhouse with a modern glass and steel structure. They fixed up the adjacent barn, adding a reception area, lounge, and catering kitchen. In the back, under the greenhouse hoops of a large garden, they created fifteen guest rooms with private patios and firepits.

As they rebranded, they began attracting a different clientele. Sally says, "It was all about making connections in our budding community, with travel sites, like And North and Escape Brooklyn; local maker markets, like the Black Barn and Field + Supply fairs; local magazines like *Upstate Diary* and *Dveight*; and all these other budding retail and hospitality platforms. None of us had big budgets, so we supported each other through word of mouth and by reposting each other on Instagram."

In late 2019, unaware of the imminent arrival of COVID-19, Sally and Doug bought another historic property in Wallkill, New York. Old Mill is a three-story home with two guest cottages, a workshop, and a barn, set on a knoll and overlooking a large pond. "Because of the pandemic, we had time to do some beautiful, labor-intensive things like the copper backsplash in the kitchen, the tall ceilings in the loft apartment, and the pergola up on the hill," Sally says.

Their lives are like a beehive where home, work, play, family, friends, and collaborators are all part of one large circular way of life. Some people who first came as guests bought their own properties, became neighbors, lifelong friends, and sometimes even associates, like Anna and Tom (pages 93–111), who were one of the first guests at Audrey's Farmhouse and went on to create the Livingstone Manor Fly-Fishing Club around the same time that Sally and Doug built the Greenhouses. Anna and Tom are transitioning from hospitality to home design, so they sold the Livingstone Manor Fly-Fishing Club to Sally and Doug. "They've already created such beauty, and it's such an iconic destination," Sally says. "We're super excited."

BREA

When peaches are in season, Doug makes peach pie for the breakfast feast. He uses butter and shortening for his dough and adds a touch of cinnamon and lemon juice to the sliced peach mix.

After Sally and Doug built a new greenhouse following the footprint of the old one, they devised a handsome, adjustable sail system to stop the interior spaces from getting too hot.

For the guest rooms, Sally cuts and arranges sea sonal wildflowers from the yard and garden in ar eclectic collection of ceramic vases, enhancin the spaces with her personal touch.

Like most of their weddings, a floral designer created this romantic, well-dressed aisle following guidance from the bride and using local, in-season flowers, grasses, and other greenery.

The bride and her entourage stay in the homey comfort of Audrey's Farmhouse, where they relax and get ready, before the bride walks down the aisle in a small courtyard adjacent to the greenhouse.

Apple cider doughnuts—baked in the oven anc topped with crunchy cinnamon and a dusting c powdered sugar—are a breakfast staple. The bat ter is flavored with apple cider, cinnamon, clove and ginger.

Staging and Hosting

The runaway success of Audrey's Farmhouse is due to Sally and Doug's endless enthusiasm, immaculate taste, and attention to detail. They take both promises of bed-and-breakfast to a whole new level. The beds—mattresses, sheets, pillows, and comforters—inspire the most cozy, comforting sleep. And breakfast, home cooked by Doug, is spectacular: homemade bread and cider doughnuts, stacks of pancakes with fresh berries, thick and fluffy Belgian waffles with local maple syrup, meat and fruit pies, zucchini or pumpkin bread, espresso chocolate chip cookies, local organic thick-cut bacon, kale hash, and flavored yogurt with rich granola and local honey. The success of the original Audrey's Farmhouse was largely due to the "we love dogs" policy, which wasn't common when they first opened in the eighties. People came from afar and kept returning. When Sally and Doug took over, the guest profile may have changed, but the presence of pets did not.

Events at the Greenhouses, mainly weddings, are also beautifully planned and executed. Though local florists create the flower arrangements, Doug supervises all the cooking, which is done in their own commercial kitchen.

Sally and Doug have changed the furniture at Audrey's Farmhouse over the years, replacing personal heirlooms with antique and vintage pieces bought from local sellers, like Ron Sharkey in Stone Ridge (see pages 69–91), fairs, and flea markets. Because of the pandemic, Old Mill was almost entirely furnished from online sources like Craigslist, eBay, and Etsy. Doug, a problem solver, has fixed and built many things himself.

Sally relies on her personal taste, her experience as a visual merchandiser, and her British heritage when she chooses pieces for the rooms. She often balances old with new, classic with quirky, nostalgia with comfort, and simplicity with coziness, as she strives to make each space feel like the country home people dream about. Working fires—like stoves, firepits, or fireplaces—and nearby stacks of wood are key to giving a warm, beating heart to each unit.

MILDRED'S LANE

J. Morgan Puett

The lane to Mildred's Lane winds through half a mile of forest, passing an old quarry and a swath of trees that a tornado recently destroyed. Newcomers describe the long driveway as an initiation, a portal, and even a consciousness-shifting experience but, for regulars, the rough ride is merely something to grumble about. Everyone agrees that the mystery, anticipation, and potholes, are part of the charm of Mildred's Lane.

The main house sits like an enchanted dacha at the end of the driveway, on the edge of rolling fields. The blackened hemlock structure uses the footprint of a former chicken coop. It was finished in 2007, ten years after artist and clothing designer J. Morgan Puett; her then partner, artist Mark Dion; and Renée Green and Nils Norman, two artist friends, bought the ninety-six-acre farmstead on the Pennsylvania banks of the Upper Delaware River.

A 1997 photoshoot shows Morgan and Mark in a large, artfully furnished canvas platform tent on the property, long before glamping was invented. Morgan had "hooshed" the space—her word for styling her environment to be beautiful and useful. Since then, they have fixed up several structures on the property: a horse shed, a large barn, and the original farmhouse, where Mildred Steffens, the lane's namesake, was born and lived her entire life until her death in 1986. Over time, artists and friends have left their own imprint on the lane with various environmental installations, including a corncrib, a treehouse, a nature shack like Thoreau's cabin, a reinvented pond, and a field of wildflowers sown from the back of a vintage pick-up truck. Each of the collaborations is unique and spans several seasons or even years.

Morgan, the only one of the four partners who still lives at the lane, runs the Mildred's Lane pedagogical project, which was described early on as "an art practice where things happen in collaboration. An experimental place for mingling ideas about architecture and environmental art." The focus was on swapping standard studio customs for the infinite canvas of nature, for and with their artist friends. Over time, the program has evolved into what Morgan defines as a "critical system aesthetics based on the history of women's work, a sustainable practice, and a rigorous engagement with every aspect of life. It is any practitioner's making-thinking-doing process." In the routine lexicon of the lane, this ritual is called "workstyles," which can be described as what happens when domestic labor like cooking, cleaning, mending, hooshing, and gardening is practiced as an art form and creates an intentional dialogue between fellows, mentors, visiting artists, scholars, and Morgan herself.

Ten years after purchasing the property, Morgan, Mark, and their son Grey Rabbit Puett moved into the 3,200-square-foot house that Morgan designed. In alignment with Morgan's radical aesthetic, the house doesn't have drywall, paint, or baseboard and trim around the doors, floors, or ceilings. Interior barn doors are made from horizontally slatted wood, and the sleeping porch is screened with a similar treatment of slatted wood.

The entry side of the house has a rusting steel wall, and the interior walls and ceilings are made from blue steel, which was darkened with the same chemical that is used for antiquing jewelry and subsequently sealed with linseed oil. The steel staircase, more sculptural than practical, floats out from a narrow steel beam with steps that are cut in random sizes and shapes.

Eclectic collections of art, antiques, books, stuffed birds, skulls, nature jars, drawings, and ephemera fill the house. Both a private family space and a public multipurpose environment, the main floor is "a central community kitchen and reference library," says Morgan. The kitchen, dining area, and covered porch contain hand-hammered metal tables and chairs, as well as comfy vintage fauteuils. Stitched-together leather hides serve as floor coverings, and antique china pieces stack up in tall metal shelves. High narrow windows on both sides of the kitchen evoke the feeling of socializing in a chapel.

EXCUSE THE
INSTALLATION
IN PROGRESS

COMING HOME
COMING HOME

PATRIOTS
Museum Legs
BARN

Social Saturdays begin with sorting the large collection of china, silver, glassware, and linens at hooshing stations. Morgan's large collection of tableware consists of heirlooms and found treasures, matching only in vintage character but making a unified design statement.

Availability of ingredients at local organic farms drives the multicourse menus. Other factors include fermentation, foraging, color palettes, and cuisine. After meals, guests wash their own dishes at a washing station.

Dinners follow a barn lecture. The table setting are like installation art, where plates, knives, fork and napkins become unconventional setting Soup might be served in teacups, hors d'oeuvre skewered on antique hatpins, and wine poured mason jars.

Guests are an eclectic mix of fellows, scholars, lecturers, farmers, crafters, artists, and designers, both local and visiting from afar. Dinner conversation varies on a multitude of topics, from backyard organic farming and foraging to natural dye processes, fracking, and politics.

A sculptural bonfire at the end of each summer session represents the conceptual completion and destruction of what was before. Often staged by artist Amy Yoes, who designs and crafts a controlled fire built in graphic layers of wood, it burns in different stages and patterns.

Events and performances after dinner—inspire by costume, music, poetry, theater, dance, an spectacle—usually take place in the barn, althoug the forest, the field, and the quarry are all possibl locations for theatrical afterparties and concerts

Workstyles

Mildred's Lane reinvents traditional notions of domestic work and life, replacing them with the concept that the act of reconsidering daily experiences can be an expression of art. Something as simple as washing bedding and making up a bed, when done with creative intention, can be as enjoyable as the ritual of slipping between the cool, crisp sheets. When sitting down with friends for a meal, it is not the beginning of a dinner party but the final act of a creative and collaborative venture. Inviting guests, planning the menu, finding and buying the ingredients, hooshing the house, choosing flowers and tableware, setting the table, cooking, serving, and generating conversation—the entire process is an artful expression. "The site-specific language that we call workstyles has evolved through experimental activities," Morgan says. "Workstyles is our engagement with life, our relations to each other, and to the site itself." These expressions of workstyles can be found all over Mildred's Lane and at the Mildred Complex(ity), the offshoot gallery and project space on Narrowsburg's Main Street.

A unique vocabulary is another result of this practice. For example, Morgan, who serves as the institutional director, is the Ambassador of Entanglement. Masters of Applied Complex(ity) are artists who build, repair, and maintain the experimental architecture. The Ministry of Comfort contributes to sustainable household methods. Cooking is called digestion choreography, turning everyday meals into a collaborative performance that equally mixes foraging, gastronomy, installation art, and social practice. And then there is hooshing. "It's a form of conceptually charged styling, cleaning, and arranging that heightens engagement with the environment," Morgan explains.

After fifteen years of evolution, Mildred's Lane is entering its next incarnation. Like other experimental communities before it, the lane tries to break free from conventional social practices. These efforts are meant to replace old with new and eventually create a new paradigm. With many new expressions of community taking place upriver, Morgan is poised to reinvent the archetype once more.

THE
OUTSIDE
INSTITUTE

INSIDE OUTSIDE

Laura Chávez Silverman and George Billard

Over the past fifteen years, Laura Chávez Silverman, a creative director, and George Billard, a filmmaker, have slowly transitioned from successful careers in New York City to rural life in Eldred, a hamlet on the New York side of the Delaware River. Laura and George met in 2005, a few weeks after Laura closed on her country home. Initially, they spent a lot of time traveling together to places like Japan, India, Laos, and Cambodia, often for George's film projects.

Laura first came to the Upper Delaware River area with her friend Scott Newkirk, the original owner of the now famous off-the-grid cabin on the cover of the book *Cabin Porn: Inspiration for Your Quiet Place Somewhere* (2015). A few years after a deal for a cabin across the creek from Scott fell through, she found her current home. "It needed some cosmetic work, but it was cute and had solid bones," she says. After Laura and George moved in, Scott designed a large, screened porch; a handyman built it; they gained a large three-season room (with a boulder in the middle); and the cabin doubled in size.

As part of her transition to living in the country, Laura wrote a blog called "Glutton for Life," where she shared experiences and recipes from her new life; reflections on how to live in nature and explore its ability to nourish; and lifestyle tips, from finding peace of mind to mixing cocktails that use homegrown and foraged herbs. Making use of her bold, exploratory recipes, she partnered with a friend and made plans to open a restaurant that reflected the spirit of "Glutton for Life"—adventurous, healthy food that was locally sourced. When the plan fell through, Laura struggled to reconnect to a sense of purpose in her surroundings, as if nature was challenging her to look deeper into herself.

By winter 2016, she was meditating every day. "One day, I opened my eyes in meditation and said, 'Oh, it's called the outside institute,'" she says. She was foreseeing a way to share her knowledge of the local ecology—the plants, fungi, birds, and trees—that she had acquired over ten years. "Like everything, we need to learn to really feel part of this world," she says. During her journey of discovery, she set out to identify and make recipes with the wild mushrooms that grew in the woods around her house. She connected with two local herbalists and mycologists, Richard Mandelbaum and Nathaniel Whitmore, who mentored her in locating edible fungi like the black trumpet mushroom, hen of the woods, and chicken of the woods. "It was a slippery slope to learn about all the rest of the ecology because, really, to be a good forager, you have to understand what grows with what, which ecosystems each one depends on, and during what season."

When Laura started the Outside Institute in 2017, her intention was to connect people with the transformative powers of nature. Initially, she was reluctant to call herself an expert. "I was largely self-taught, but I met so many curious people who wanted to learn more about nature that I decided to teach what I know," she says.

By 2019, Laura and George were part of a group that started the Barryville farmers market, where they developed relationships with local farmers. When the supply chain faltered during the pandemic, George started a service that delivered produce from regional farms to households in the city. "One-click overnight delivery over long distances is just not sustainable in the long run," George says. "We learned that the way forward is to support our local economies, like regional farms, and eat local, in-season food."

Laura's evolution from cautious to committed upriver resident deepened further when she opened the Outside Institute storefront in Callicoon, New York. The stylish outpost offers workshops that range from making tinctures and dyeing with local plants to preserving wild-foraged ingredients and coping with tick-borne diseases. It also sells the institute's merchandise, like wild mushroom salt, a Reishi tincture, and her three-part *Field Guide to the Northeast*. "There's even a space in the back where I can craft local goods," she says.

& ANTARCTICA
& AFRICA
OCEANIA

Edward Weston Forms of Passion
Blossfeldt
OUTDOORS
PLANTING

CHIOT

Axe Handbook
INDIA
a change of appetite
DIANA HENRY
OTTOLENGHI
NATURAL TABLES
ATLAS

WOODCUT
The Crossley Guide
BIRDS OF THE WORLD
EUROPE & AFRICA
ASIA & OCEANIA

A spring salad of radicchio, foraged pickled ramps, locally smoked trout, local organic egg, micro-greens, and crispy shallots looks beautiful in a handmade bowl by ceramicist Mirena Kim.

Laura's three-part *Field Guide to the Northeast* provides an accessible introduction to the region's most prevalent flora, fauna, and fungi, with recipes highlighting wild flavors of spring, summer, fall, and winter.

Fall tinctures from Laura's kitchen, including a ros wine aperitif infused with Japanese knotweed an spices, and a cure-all made of apple cider vinega infused with citrus, herbs, chilis, and horseradish

The seeds of the bull thistle (*Cirsium vulgare*), a naturalized plant whose vivid purple flowers provide nectar for many pollinator species. The seeds are eaten by finches and the downy fluff serves to line their nests.

Laura teaches that foraging sustainably means being mindful of the insects, birds, and other creatures who rely on what you extract, and educated interaction with the land is most important.

Monarch butterflies, an endangered species, de pend on milkweed, which is indigenous to Nort America. You can help Monarch butterfly propa gation by planting milkweed.

Sustainable Foraging

Laura's Outside Institute outpost in Callicoon, New York, offers nature walks that explore the landscape and ecosystems of the Upper Delaware River and Hudson River Valley. The "forest immersion walk" is based on the Japanese practice of *shinrin-yoku*—the simple act of walking mindfully through the woods—and encourages a slowing of the breath and engagement of all the senses, generating a positive impact on health and well-being. Foraging walks are an opportunity to discover wild edibles in season, while Laura teaches identification skills and offers knowledge about where and how to forage. "I seek out anomalies in the landscape," she says about her foraging technique. "I blur my vision, allowing my eye to catch whatever sticks out as different in the vastness of the forest."

Laura suggests that, to connect with the transformative powers of nature, it is important to become mindful of where you live and where to forage. Find out where to go, when to hike, what to look for, what to take, and what to leave alone. Immerse yourself in nature by slowing down to a point where you're aware not of the silence but of the sounds that surround you. Nature is abundant with edibles that can sustain and even heal us, like mushrooms, edible plants, and weeds, and even the bark of trees. To forage responsibly, respect every plant population you encounter. For example, ramps are wild leeks and can be extracted in the spring; they are bulbs and benefit from being thinned out. Taking every single one, however, destroys the chance of a harvest the following year. When starting a foraging expedition, it's essential to know what you're looking for. Beginner foragers will benefit from a guide, who can help with locating and identifying edible greens and mushrooms.

The Outside Institute outpost also hosts wildcrafting workshops such as herbalism, to make herbal tinctures with locally harvested plants; dyeing with plants, to use native plants to dye natural fabrics; botanical mixology, to muddle, mix, and shake up cocktails and mocktails using botanical tinctures made with local and wild-foraged ingredients; and cooking wild foods, to cook simple, healthy meals with foraged edible plants.

UPCYCLED CABIN

Bette Blau and Steve Randazzo

Following a Thanksgiving holiday in Eldred, New York, and after several years of weekending at friends' houses Upstate, Bette Blau said to her husband, "Steve, I don't want to be a guest anymore. I really would love to have our own weekend house."

Soon after, in 2005, Bette and Steve—who work as a photography team, creating lush images of food, still life, and more—met with a real estate broker, who had planned a day of viewings along the banks of the Delaware River. When they pulled into the driveway of the second house on the list, Bette turned to Steve and blurted out, "I'm home!" She recalls that "it just seemed the most natural reaction." As they walked up to the brown shingle cabin, they realized it was hardly impressive. "The real estate broker kept saying 'It's so small, it's so small,'" Steve says, "but we're from Manhattan; we know how to do small." They had no doubt: the tiny, neglected, and drafty cabin was destined to be theirs. "We made the decision because of the large pond too," Bette says. "It was just so beautiful."

They got to work right away. Steve enclosed the front porch to create a mudroom and insulated the walls as best he could. The original cabin had two bedrooms; their sons, Marley and Julian, slept upstairs, and Bette and Steve slept downstairs. "It felt more secure that way," Bette says. "We were just so isolated." Early on, Bette did worry about an intruder. One day, a bear ripped up a foraged honeycomb that she had left on the stairs. "I was like, 'Who broke into our house?'" she says. Later, another bear ravaged the garbage, so they put a lock on the lean-to shed. The bear returned a few days later, lifted the entire structure, and dragged it toward the woods, taking the garbage with him.

As they got accustomed to living alongside nature's creatures, elements of professional life shifted. Bette, a visual artist who was a prop stylist for many years, eventually focused on smaller and more intentional projects, like a blog about collecting and creating in nature, and art direction for chefs and artisans. Steve maintained his personal clients, often traveling throughout the country for shoots, and relished coming home to the woods, the pond, and the house.

In the early years of living in the country, Bette and Steve started thinking about expanding the house and building a studio "like a compound for the entire family," Steve says. But it wasn't until March 2020 that they were finally set to break ground. "Ours was the last building permit that the county issued before the pandemic lockdown," Steve says.

As most building sites were shutting down, Bette and Steve gained access to a great construction team who helped them make bold design decisions. Sensing they might be in the country indefinitely, and because life was mainly taking place outdoors, they doubled the size of the screened-in porch. During this unusual time, visiting friends had good insights too, like an interior designer who took one look at the standard kitchen island and proposed to double its size and rotate it 180 degrees. "She was only here because of COVID," Bette says, "and her suggestion changed the feel of the whole downstairs."

For the 1,500-square-foot addition, which would include a studio and two upstairs bedrooms, they settled on a prefab design by Grey's Woodworks. First, they built the foundation, and then a crane lifted four prefabricated walls onto four corner posts. "The rest took maybe another four weeks," says Bette.

As the world slowly returns to normal, Bette explains that their homelife in the summer is still centered on the porch. In fall, they shut the doors to the porch and life moves to the kitchen island and fireplace. In winter, only the barrel sauna by the edge of the water gets people out of the house and into nature. Some courageous friends may even jump into the freezing pond.

ENDICOTT JOHNSON
CROWN DISTRIBUTION
CENTER

↑
STUDIO

FIRE
EXTINGUISHER
Six Seasons
JERUSALEM
HOW TO GRILL VEGETABLES
Grains for
Every Season

46 TO KINGS HIGHWAY
46 TO CHURCH AVE
46 TO BROADWAY
46 TO FULTON ST
46 TO EASTERN PKWAY
46 TO WASHINGTON PLAZA
46 TO AVENUE N
49 TO BERGEN ST
49 TO SHORE BLVD
TO AVENUE U
PROPERTY OF
AMERICAN STORES CO.
KEARNY, N.J.
BANANA BOX
RETURN TO WAREHOUSE PROMPTLY

Fire
MANA

Abandoned bird's nests found in late fall or winter can make great art pieces, especially ones with eggs in them, like these bright blue robin's eggs. Never remove a nest in the spring as it may be under construction or in use.

Forager's art workshops end with a photography session, where Bette shows participants how to use natural light to shoot a compelling tableau of artfully arranged elements from nature.

To make the best prints of mushroom spores, th tiny reproductive cells in the underside gills, use flat mushroom with an open cap and exposed gill remove the stem, place bottom down on colore paper, and leave for six to twelve hours.

The images taken in Laura and Bette's workshops are often whimsical and abstract. They not only explore a connection to the environment but also discover the individual elements in nature.

Bette's art relies on synchronicity, repetition, and finding a balance between color, shape, texture, and mass. Repeating a single type of object—like a pine cone, a shell, or the spores of a mushroom—often creates a powerful reaction to an image.

While walking through the woods, Bette inspire an artful eye by encouraging workshop partic ipants to seek out things they've never notice before, like looking through a microscope for th first time, and to deeply consider what they find.

Nature = Art

Human expression developed not only from observation of nature, but also from experimentation with natural materials like chalk, stone, and wood.

For her visual art practice, Bette is an avid collector of discarded objects with history, character, and beauty in corroded, broken, or changed states. While Bette was living in the city, the objects of her fascination were often man-made, like kitchen utensils, pottery, and industrial components. When Bette moved to the country, she started hiking with Laura Chávez Silverman (see pages 197–213) and began seeing nature more closely and more clearly. Her collecting shifted to include things from her immediate environment like seed pods, nests, twigs, skulls, and mushrooms. The resulting graphic compositions echoed her previous work but with a different eye, newly introduced to detect nuance and beauty in objects from nature.

"Collecting is really about training your eye," says Bette. "At a flea market, I spot things that people don't. Laura helped me do the same in nature."

Laura and Bette host the Outside Institute's forager's art workshops, which begin at Bette's studio. There, Laura explains the rule to extract mindfully: only take what you need, be sensitive to animal habitat, and leave little trace. The walk takes a little over an hour and, by the end, each participant holds a small collection of found objects—from wildflowers and grasses to seed pods, small rocks, twigs, and pine cones. Back in the studio, Bette explains the power of repetition, be it in shape, color, or texture, and encourages finding harmony between the objects when creating the layout. She explains that simplifying and reduction often lead to the right balance.

To create a photograph of everyone's tableaux, Bette uses natural light that streams in through the studio window, mounts an iPhone on a tripod, and photographs the arrangements from about twenty inches away. These creative gatherings enjoyed in community offer artful and rewarding experiences that foster appreciation for the ultimate compositions: those created by nature itself.

SCHOOL OF COLOR

Diane Townsend and Judah Catalan

In fall 1985, while she was shopping for produce at the New York Farmers Market, a local farmer told Diane Townsend about a derelict 1851 schoolhouse that was for sale in Milanville, Wayne County, Pennsylvania. Curious and in need of a trip to the country, Diane went to see it and, with the money from a small inheritance, bought it on the spot. "It was a wreck. It hadn't been used since 1963," she says. She cleared out the garbage, demolished some walls, built others, installed a central staircase with a mezzanine, and eventually created the bedroom loft that takes up the top floor of the building. She removed the teacher's lectern and gave the recitation bench to her daughter, Wendy. She preserved the original blackboards and wooden wainscoting, which she painted in a celadon green that she created herself from the same pigments she uses for the pastels she makes.

When Diane was still living in SoHo, she found a dumpster full of pigments from a printing factory that was going out of business. She had been working with traditional Rembrandt pastels but found them too chalky. Her studio mate, an Italian art conservationist, knew how to craft pastels and helped with her first set. Over time, she created a dense pastel in a palette of organic colors and unique tonalities that reflect her creative spirit. Initially, she used the pastels for her own drawings and, eventually, other artists caught on. "I would make a new batch, someone would find out, and I'd sell them all," she says.

Artist Judah Catalan first met Diane at a National Arts Club event, where she was selling her Artists' Pastels. He tested them on a sheet of paper and bought a box. Struck by his formidable presence, Diane saved the sketch and pinned it on her wall. A few weeks and several dates later, Diane invited Judah to Pennsylvania. She picked him up from the bus stop in Monticello, New York, and brought him back to her studio in the schoolhouse. Judah took one look at the property and changed his dress overalls to his work overalls. (Judah has worn nothing but overalls since the seventies. He owns one in every available color and for every occasion.)

A teacher of the Alexander Technique, an alternative therapy focusing on posture and movement, Judah helped people treat and use their bodies in the way nature intended. With a similar awareness, he recognized the potential of Diane's property. "The hillside behind the schoolhouse had enormous promise," he says. Over time, Judah and Diane created a large front lawn, flower and vegetable beds, espaliered fruit trees, an aviary, and two ponds, all defined by stone walls that Judah built. "The property was dotted with enormous boulders, but there were no usable rocks," he says. He collected some rocks from Wendy and her husband Mark, who live on a farm across the Delaware River, but soon those weren't enough. "When word got out about Judah's walls, a local farmer reached out to us," Diane says. "To the farmer, the rocks in his pastures were obstacles, but for Judah they were treasures."

Over time, Judah worked on clearing rocks from the land of a dozen or so farmers. Many became friends, and each wall on Judah and Diane's land contains a story of their collaboration. "The stonework became part of the local folklore, like I was this giant with special powers. But it was really just my stubbornness that built them," Judah says.

In 2006, they gave up their place in the city, moved to Milanville, and added a studio. They modeled the new building after the old schoolhouse to create a simple counterbalance at the other end of the property. Zoned as a barn, it has no amenities; Judah's studio is on the top floor, and Diane works on the main floor. Curving steps that Judah stacked with massive stones mark the entrance. They lead to a metal bridge, which connects to the front door.

DRAWER #16
PAPER
DRAWER #17

de Kooning

Judah adds edible flowers from the garden, nasturtium and Johnny Jump Ups, to add a pop of color to salads, desserts, and cocktails. Other edible flowers include allium, marigolds, calendula, and scarlet runner beans.

Diane's pastels are shaped by hand, using ground pumice and pigments. She mixes blue ultramarine, cadmium red, yellow, orange, some violets, and earth tones to create her palette.

The colors in Judah and Diane's hillside gardens come from a variety of astilbes, rugosa roses daylilies, Japanese irises, lupines, and fox gloves, as well as berry bushes, fruit trees, herbs, and vegetables.

Diane paints in a classical abstract style. Her paintings create a moment of color in any environment. She applies her philosophy of using color in a range of one shade and adding accents.

A bowl of peaches adds color to a windowsill. Fruits such as oranges, plums, peaches, or red apples create color accents around the house, placed in spots that catch the sunlight.

Judah's stuffed zucchini blossoms—filled with a paste of zucchini, mushrooms, chives, and goat cheese—are a bright accent in the kitchen, but once cooked turn a muted ochre.

Playing with Color

Diane began making her Artists' Pastels in the seventies, using a seventeenth-century Italian formula. Since then, she and Judah have refined them into smooth, easy-to-use materials that are as rich in pigment as possible. They shape their pastels by hand, rolling and compressing the particles—pigment, pumice, and binder—in a mix that gives exceptional flow and permanence. Diane creates the colors in the collection instinctively, based on her personal experience as an artist. Her palette reflects the way we see colors in real life. They are muted, distinct, and comforting, with accents in fluorescent and metallic shades.

Though she works with color every day, Diane doesn't wear many colorful clothes. "I like neutrals and subtle colors with an occasional bright accent, but I don't wear colorful prints," she says. Diane suggests using colors as if they are rare and expensive, and you can only afford two or three. "Stay within a certain range, like shades of one color, with perhaps one accent because our capacity to take in more successfully is rather iffy," says Diane.

Those principles are everywhere throughout Diane's life. The colors of the schoolhouse follow the shades-of-one-color rule, like several hues of bluish green, celadon, and sage that act as accent colors to the white walls. In her atelier, depending on when you visit, her paintings are also in shades of one color, with the occasional accent. Judah uses color instinctively in his art, which includes wire sculptures in electric hues and vivid pastel drawings. And when he cooks, his delicate dishes range in color from stunningly subtle to vibrant, like yellow zucchini blossoms served with red tomatoes and green salads dotted with bright flowers. Bowls of fruit and bouquets throughout the house represent the many colors from the gardens and, in all their splendor, the accent colors.

In the summer, the hillside gardens are abundant with flowers of all colors, and the air is abuzz with butterflies, hummingbirds, and bees. "We did research and planted butterfly- and bee-attracting plants," Judah says. Water from two ponds also attracts the pollinators, but the couple does not keep apiaries. "The bees spend all day here, going from flower to flower," Diane says, "and then they go elsewhere to make their honey."

ACKNOWLEDGMENTS

From late March 2020 through the rest of the year, my family and I spent almost every Saturday night at Mildred's Lane (page 173) by a large open fire, grilling, eating, and catching up with friends, while socially distanced. It felt a bit clandestine and often we were freezing, but it didn't matter. Socializing had never been more intimate. Perhaps because those evenings were like forbidden fruit, they will stay with me forever. The knowledge that we were not alone and all over the region people were enjoying the same thing made me curious about their experiences, their homes, their creative solutions. I started making lists of places and gatherings that looked yummy. Eventually, I began pitching the idea of this book, asking total strangers if I could come and intrude in their homes and lives. Some said, "No, thank you. Our house is such a mess after two years of intense occupation." But most welcomed me with open arms, treating me like the new friend we would soon become.

These collaborations with the creative pioneers featured here made this book possible. Thank you to Julie and Peter, Nadia and John, Elizabeth and Jake, Ron, Anna and Tom, Todd and Carter, Sally and Doug, Morgan, Laura and George, Bette and Steve, Diane and Judah, and Carin and James! Heartbreakingly, Carin Goldberg passed away on January 19, 2023. "Graphic Farmstead" (page 113) is dedicated to her memory.

This book was merely a dream without the support of Rizzoli, and I am beyond grateful to publisher Charles Miers and editor Daniel Melamud for publishing *Living Upriver: Artful Homes, Idyllic Lives*. I am honored by the enthusiastic words of Emma Austen Tuccillo, a champion of creative people and their endeavors Upstate and in the Upper Delaware River area. I thank Alastair, my husband and partner of thirty-three years, who has shown me how to make beautiful books, leading me from the world of fashion to the world of publishing. I thank my four lovely and talented children: Kiki, for her graphic design and creating the stick font for the title; Leila, for helping with scouting and photography; and Iona and Iain, for their fresh eye and feedback. And last but not least, I dedicate this book to my mother, Bieneke Roelofs. Thank you for a lifetime of love and support.

ABOUT:

Barbara de Vries is the author of *Coming Home: Modern Rustic, Creative Living in Dutch Interiors* (Rizzoli, 2021), and *Stupid Model: In Paris and Down Under* (GdeV Studio, 2016). She has designed numerous lifestyle books on architecture, design, fashion, and food. Barbara began her career in fashion as a model in Paris and went on to study fashion design at the Royal College of Art in London. In 1990, she moved to New York, where she became the senior design director at Calvin Klein and helped create the iconic CK brand. She subsequently had her own collections in the United States and Japan. In 2009, Barbara and her husband, author Alastair Gordon, launched Gordon de Vries Studio. Together, they create illustrated books on design and lifestyle.

Emma Austen Tuccillo is the founder and creative director of And North, a curated guide to Upstate New York. Through travel recommendations and unique events, And North inspires city dwellers and locals alike to explore the beautiful regions north of New York City while helping small businesses to grow and thrive.

PHOTO CREDITS:

Principal photography: Barbara de Vries
Page 1, 2: Kiki Gordon
Page 7: Leila Gordon
Page 170, top left and bottom right: Sally Hutchinson
Page 179, top left: Alastair Gordon
Page 190, top left, right: Leila Gordon
Page 190, bottom left: Alastair Gordon
Page 195: Alastair Gordon
Page 226, top left and right: Bette Blau
Page 226, bottom center: Bette Blau
Page 227: Bette Blau
Page 236: top right: Leila Gordon
Page 237: top left: Leila Gordon
Page 253: Bette Blau

ART:

Page 219: painting by © Justin Lyons
Back cover: Birch Bark painting by © Kiki Gordon

PLACES:

Cover: The fireplace room at Nadia and Doug's house, chapter "Hand Hewn" (page 33).
Pages 4–5: Living room at Anna Aberg and Tom Roberts' house, chapter "Upstate Swedish" (page 93).
Page 7: Outdoor table setting at J. Morgan Puett's place, chapter "Mildred's Lane" (page 173).
Pages 8–9: The Ravenwood barn in Kerhonkson, New York, is a popular summer destination created by Chris Lanier and Dana McClure.
Pages 250–251: The view of the Upper Delaware river, photographed from the lawn at Seminary Hill, a hotel, restaurant, and cidery in Callicoon, New York.

First published in the United States of America in 2023 by
Rizzoli International Publications, Inc.
300 Park Avenue South
New York, NY 10010
www.rizzoliusa.com

Instagram/cominghome.co

Publisher: Charles Miers
Editor: Daniel Melamud
Production: Kaija Markoe
Copy editor: Megan Conway
Proofreader: Cindy Trickel

ISBN: 9780847873265
Library of Congress Control Number: 2023931804

2023 2024 2025 2026 / 10 9 8 7 6 5 4 3 2 1
Printed in China

Visit us online:
Facebook.com/RizzoliNewYork
Twitter: @Rizzoli_Books
Instagram.com/RizzoliBooks
Pinterest.com/RizzoliBooks
Youtube.com/user/RizzoliNY